ESSE

D0530779

HOUSE PLANTS

ESSENTIAL TIPS 101

HOUSE PLANTS

John Brookes

DORLING KINDERSLEY
London • New York • Sydney
www.dk.com

A DORLING KINDERSLEY BOOK

Editor Irene Lyford
Art Editor Ann Thompson
DTP Designer Mark Bracey
Series Editor Charlotte Davies
Series Art Editor Clive Hayball
Production Controller Lauren Britton

First published in Great Britain in 1996 by
Dorling Kindersley Limited,
80 Strand, London WC2R 0RL

A CIP catalogue record for this book is available from the British Library

ISBN 0-7513-0280-5

Text film output by The Right Type, Great Britain
Reproduced by Colourscan, Singapore
Printed in China by WKT

E S S E N T I A L TIPS

HOUSE PLANT CHOICE

1 HOW TO SELECT A GOOD HOUSE PLANT

Opt for a vigorous-looking plant with strong stems and a good, even coverage of healthy leaves. Avoid plants with yellowing or brown-tipped leaves, and neglected specimens, with dried-out compost shrinking away from the sides of the pot or roots growing out of the bottom. If selecting a flowering plant, look for one with plenty of flower buds, and avoid those with tightly closed green buds, which often fail to open indoors.

Strong stems with even leaf coverage

Mass of unopened flower buds

Thick, succulent stems

Glossy variegated leaves

IMPATIENS ACCENT CERISE ▷

HEPTAPLEURUM ARBORICOLA △

2 EASY CARE PLANTS

All house plants require care, but some are more tolerant than others of unsuitable conditions and will survive with the minimum of attention. Such house plants are a sensible choice for beginners or for those with little time to spare for indoor gardening.

△ ZEBRINA PENDULA
This trailing plant has attractively coloured leaves.

Occasionally mist-spray leaves

△ CAMPANULA ISOPHYLLA
Delicate white or blue flowers bloom profusely throughout summer.

Repot only if roots fill pot completely; topdress older plants

△ ASPIDISTRA ELATIOR
Aspidistras tolerate poor light, some dryness, and a wide range of temperatures.

EASY CARE HOUSE PLANTS
Boston fern (*Nephrolepis exaltata* "Bostoniensis")
Cast-iron plant (*Aspidistra elatior*)
Chinese jade (*Crassula arborescens*)
Cineraria (*Senecio cruentus* hybrids)
Grape ivy (*Cissus rhombifolia*)
Italian bellflower (*Campanula isophylla*)
Mind-your-own-business (*Soleirolia soleirolii*)
Painted nettle (*Coleus blumei*)
Spider plant (*Chlorophytum comosum* "Vittatum")
Tom thumb (*Kalanchoe blossfeldiana* hybrids)
Veitch screw pine (*Pandanus veitchii*)
Wandering Jew (*Zebrina pendula*)

3 MATCHING PLANTS TO CONDITIONS

The chart below recommends the best conditions for a number of the most popular house plants:
Warm: 15°–21° C (59°–70° F);
Cool: 10°–15° C (50°–59° F);

Sunny: direct sun for part of day;
Filtered sun: direct sun, filtered through blinds or light curtains;
Shady: no direct or filtered sun, but enough light for plant growth.

Plant	Mini-climate
African violet (*Saintpaulia* hybrids)	Warm, filtered
Azalea (*Rhododendron* hybrids)	Cool, filtered
Bird's-nest fern (*Asplenium nidus*)	Warm, shady
Boston fern (*Nephrolepis exaltata* "Bostoniensis")	Warm, shady
Busy Lizzie (*Impatiens walleriana* hybrids)	Warm, sunny
Cast-iron plant (*Aspidistra elatior*)	Cool, filtered
Croton (*Codiaeum variegatum pictum*)	Warm, sunny
English ivy (*Hedera helix* hybrids)	Cool, filtered
Florist's cyclamen (*Cyclamen persicum* hybrids)	Cool, filtered
Grape ivy (*Cissus rhombifolia*)	Warm, filtered
Heartleaf philodendron (*Philodendron scandens*)	Warm, shady
Italian bellflower (*Campanula isophylla*)	Cool, sunny
Kangaroo vine (*Cissus antarctica*)	Warm, filtered
Kentia palm (*Howea belmoreana*)	Warm, filtered
Maidenhair fern (*Adiantum raddianum*)	Warm, shady
Mind-your-own-business (*Soleirolia soleirolii*)	Cool, sunny
Painted-leaf begonia (*Begonia rex-cultorum*)	Warm, shady
Painted nettle (*Coleus blumei*)	Warm, sunny
Parlour palm (*Chamaedorea elegans* "Bella")	Warm, filtered
Poinsettia (*Euphorbia pulcherrima*)	Warm, sunny
Primula (*Primula obconica*)	Cool, filtered
Regal geranium (*Pelargonium domesticum* hybrids)	Cool, sunny
Rubber plant (*Ficus elastica*)	Warm, shady
Spider plant (*Chlorophytum comosum* "Vittatum")	Cool, filtered
Swiss cheese plant (*Monstera deliciosa*)	Warm, shady
Tom Thumb (*Kalanchoe blossfeldiana* hybrids)	Warm, sunny
Tradescantia (*Tradescantia albiflora* "Albovittata")	Warm, sunny
Winter cherry (*Solanum capsicastrum*)	Cool, sunny

4 CHECKING FOR PESTS & STEM ROT

Before buying a plant, examine it closely for any signs of pests and disease to avoid contaminating the rest of your plants. Since the pests may not be visible, check also for any evidence of pest damage to the plant, for example sticky patches or distorted or mottled leaves.

CHECK FOR STEM ROT
Pull back the leaves to examine the centre of the plant for slimy or rotting leaves.

CHECK FOR PESTS & PEST DAMAGE
Look under leaves, on flowerbuds, and around growing tips of stems for pests.

5 TAKING YOUR PLANTS HOME

House plants are used to warm conditions and can be damaged by cold draughts or by sudden changes in the temperature. To minimize the risk of such damage to newly bought plants on the journey home, keep them in the plastic sleeves provided by garden centres and shops. For an extra layer of insulation, put the new plants, in their plastic sleeves, in a deep cardboard box. If you are travelling by car, wedge several plants together in the box to prevent them from falling over.

PROTECT YOUR PLANTS

6 GROWING BULBS INDOORS

A great many of the popular spring bulbs can be grown indoors in pots of bulb fibre. Buy the bulbs in autumn or early winter, checking carefully that they are firm and free from disease.

Plant the bulbs in moist bulb fibre, then leave them in a cool, dark place for several weeks, checking regularly to see if they need more water. During this essential "wintering" period, the bulbs' root systems will be established. Once shoots start to emerge, gradually bring the bulbs into the light. For early flowering, buy the specially prepared bulbs that require a shorter period of wintering before the shoots appear.

POT-GROWN SPRING FLOWERS ▽
From left to right are: Scilla, Crocus, Chionodoxa, dwarf daffodil, Puschkinia, hyacinth, and waterlily tulip. After flowering, remove flowerheads, let leaves die back, then plant the bulbs outside.

HYACINTH

DAFFODIL

NARCISSUS

TULIP

CROCUS

GRAPE HYACINTH

DWARF IRIS

SPECIES CROCUS

LIGHT & HUMIDITY

7 WHAT DO HOUSE PLANTS NEED?

In order to grow, plants need to be placed in an appropriate growing medium; watered; fed; and provided with light, heat, and humidity. They also need to be potted on as they grow and monitored for pests and disease.

House plants vary in their exact requirements, so find out what each of your plants needs and try to satisfy this as far as possible.

Leaves absorb carbon dioxide, water, and sunlight for energy and oxygen production

Roots take up water and minerals from potting mixture

LEAVES, STEM, & ROOTS OF PLANT

8 CHECK LIGHT INTENSITY

Light intensity varies not only from room to room, but also within a room, depending on the distance from a window. As the diagram illustrates, the area directly in front of the window receives most natural light. At just 2m (6 ft) into the room, the light level is 80 per cent lower. The areas on either side of the window also receive very little light.

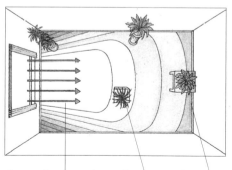

Arrows show direction of light into room from window

Area in front of window receives most natural light

Dark grey shading shows area with least natural light

13

9 TURN YOUR PLANTS

Most plants grow towards the source of light, so turn your plants often to ensure balanced growth. This is very important in rooms with dark-coloured walls that absorb the light, rather than reflect it, forcing plants to turn towards the window.

Plant grows at an angle, due to lack of regular turning

LIGHT-SEEKING *Plants grow towards the light (here* Codiaeum variegatum pictum).

10 MONITORING TEMPERATURE

Check room temperature regularly to ensure that it is suitable for your plants. Most popular house plants thrive in a temperature range of 15°–21° C (59°–70° F).

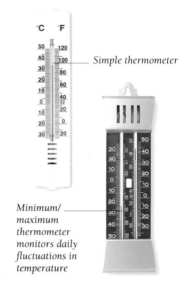

Simple thermometer

Minimum/ maximum thermometer monitors daily fluctuations in temperature

11 AVOID SCORCHING

Shade-loving plants develop brown scorched patches if exposed to intense sunlight; even sun-lovers can be damaged by an unexpected exposure, so try to acclimatize your plants gradually to brighter light.

Brown marks on the leaves indicate scorching

EPIPREMNUM AUREUM

12 WHY CHOOSE FILTERED LIGHT?

While few house plants like either direct sunlight or very poor light, filtered sunlight suits most types. This fairly high level of brightness is found 1–1.5 m (3–5 ft) from a sunny window, or near a window where direct sun filters through a curtain, blind, or a tree outside.

13 PLANTS FOR SUNNY CONDITIONS

A sunny position is one that receives direct sunlight for all or part of the day, although the strength of the sunlight will depend on the latitude, the time of year, and the orientation of the room. Such bright light suits plants like desert cacti, succulents, hard-leaved bromeliads, and certain sun-loving flowering plants.

Glossy leaves

△ PASSION FLOWER
Prune heavily in spring to retain the shape.

Dark green spiky leaves

◁ HIBISCUS
Place on a sunny windowsill for a succession of colourful flowers.

Clumps of leaves grow from trunk-like stem

◁ YUCCA
Keep a yucca in direct sunlight throughout the year.

SUN-LOVING HOUSE PLANTS
Black-eyed Susan (*Thunbergia alata*)
Chinese hibiscus (*Hibiscus rosa-sinensis*)
Claw cactus (*Schlumbergera truncata*)
Earth star plant (*Cryptanthus biviattatus*)
Lace aloe (*Aloe aristata*)
Passion flower (*Passiflora caerulea*)
Poinsettia (*Euphorbia pulcherrima*)
Silver vine (*Scindapsus pictus* "Argyraeus")
Spineless yucca (*Yucca elephantipes*)
Swedish ivy (*Plectranthus australis*)
Urn plant (*Aechmea fasciata*)
Wax flower (*Stephanotis floribunda*)

14 PLANTS FOR SHADY CONDITIONS

A shady position is a moderately lit area, perhaps 1.5–2 m (5–6 ft) from a sunny window, along a side wall, or near a sunless window. The light in this situation may not be adequate for plants in the shorter winter days.

SHADE-TOLERANT HOUSE PLANTS
Angel wings (*Caladium hortulanum* hybrids)
Bird's nest fern (*Asplenium nidus*)
Burgundy philodendron (*Philodendron* "Burgundy")
Button fern (*Pellaea rotundifolia*)
Hare's foot fern (*Polypodium aureum* "Mandaianum")
Herringbone plant (*Maranta leuconeura erythroneura*)
Maidenhair fern (*Adiantum raddianum*)
Peace lily (*Spathiphyllum* "Clevelandii")
Peacock plant (*Calathea makoyana*)
Spotted dumb cane (*Dieffenbachia exotica*)
Staghorn fern (*Platycerium bifurcatum*)
Weeping fig (*Ficus benjamina*)

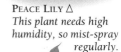

PEACE LILY △
This plant needs high humidity, so mist-spray regularly.

HERRINGBONE PLANT ▽
The vivid colours of the leaves will fade if exposed to too bright light.

SPOTTED DUMB CANE ▷
Keep this plant with poisonous sap well away from children.

Small, heart-shaped leaves

Delicate, thread-like stems

ROSARY VINE ▷
If this plant is not grown in direct sunlight, leaf colouring fades and growth is leggy.

GOLDEN BARREL CACTUS ▽
Do not water during the plant's winter rest period.

$\underline{15}$ PLANTS FOR DRY ATMOSPHERES

A dry environment is one in which the amount of water vapour in the air is very low, and often occurs in winter in centrally heated homes. Apart from cacti and other succulents, which are adapted to dry conditions, few house plants can tolerate this situation.

Fan-shaped leaves with thin silvery bloom

SILVER CROWN ▷
Feed this succulent with liquid fertilizer during the active growing season.

HOUSE PLANTS FOR DRY ENVIRONMENTS
Bishop's cap (*Astrophytum myriostigma*)
Fish-hook cactus (*Ferocactus latispinus*)
Golden barrel cactus (*Echinocactus grusonii*)
Golden pincushion (*Mammillaria rhodantha*)
Moulded wax plant (*Echevaria agavoides*)
Painted lady (*Echeveria derenbergii*)
Queen agave (*Agave victoriae-reginae*)
Rabbit's ears cactus (*Opuntia microdasys*)
Rat's tail cactus (*Aporocactus flagelliformis*)
Rosary vine (*Ceropegia woodii*)
Rose pincushion (*Mammillaria zeilmanniana*)
Silver crown (*Cotyledon undulata*)

16 SPOT HUMIDITY DEFICIENCY

Few house plants can tolerate
a dry atmosphere, but those
with thin leaves, such as ferns,
are most vulnerable. They will
display the following symptoms:
- Leaf tips turn brown and shrivel.
- Flowers and flower buds drop.
- Leaves start to wilt or drop.

MAIDENHAIR FERN
*Dry air has caused
the leaves of this fern
to shrivel and die.*

MIST-SPRAY DAILY WITH TEPID WATER
*As well as increasing humidity, misting
keeps plants clean and discourages pests.*

17 HOW TO INCREASE HUMIDITY LEVELS

Apart from investing in an electric
humidifier, there are several simple
strategies for increasing humidity
around plants. Grouping plants is a
simple and effective method as the
moisture transpired by one plant
increases the humidity
around its neighbour.

BURY POTS IN WATER-RETENTIVE MIXTURE
*A mix of peat-substitute and vermiculite is
ideal for this method of raising humidity.*

STAND PLANTS ON MOIST PEBBLE TRAY
*Keep the pebbles moist and the water will
evaporate into the air around the plants.*

18 HIGH HUMIDITY LOVERS

Although most house plants prefer a moderate degree of humidity, there are some for whom high humidity levels are essential. These include thin-leaved plants such as maidenhair fern (*Adiantum raddianum*) and painted nettles (*Coleus blumei*). Such plants are particularly at risk in winter in homes with central heating.

◁ PEPEROMIA
Stand this plant on a moist pebble tray, but do not mist-spray.

FATSIA JAPONICA ▷
This fast-growing plant reaches 1.2 m (4 ft). Mist-spray the foliage frequently.

STEPHANOTIS ▽
Stand this vigorous climber on a moist pebble tray. Decrease watering in winter.

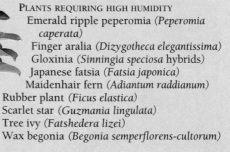

PLANTS REQUIRING HIGH HUMIDITY
Emerald ripple peperomia (*Peperomia caperata*)
Finger aralia (*Dizygotheca elegantissima*)
Gloxinia (*Sinningia speciosa* hybrids)
Japanese fatsia (*Fatsia japonica*)
Maidenhair fern (*Adiantum raddianum*)
Rubber plant (*Ficus elastica*)
Scarlet star (*Guzmania lingulata*)
Tree ivy (*Fatshedera lizei*)
Wax begonia (*Begonia semperflorens-cultorum*)

WATERING KNOW-HOW

19 HOW MUCH WATER?

House plants vary in their watering requirements, depending on their size, type, environment, and the time of year. It is important to give the right amount of water, as both under- and overwatering can seriously damage plants.

Instructions to "water plentifully" indicate that the potting mixture should be kept moist at all times and that the surface should not be allowed to dry out. When watering plentifully, continue pouring until water flows out through the holes at the bottom of the container.

To water sparingly, provide just enough water to barely moisten the potting mixture throughout.

Plants to water sparingly
- Plants in the winter rest period.
- Those with thick, fleshy roots.
- Thick, leathery-leaved plants.
- Plants in plastic or glazed pots.
- Succulent plants, such as cacti.
- Plants in bottle gardens and terraria.

Plants needing plentiful watering
- Actively growing house plants.
- Those with budding leaves and flowers about to bloom.
- Plants with delicate thin leaves.
- Large-leaved plants that clearly transpire a lot of water.
- Plants in relatively small pots.
- Any plants growing in a very warm room or a dry atmosphere.
- Plants from bogs and marshy areas: e.g. umbrella plants.
- Those in unglazed clay pots.
- Plants growing in free-draining potting mixtures, including peat.

◁ FICUS BENJAMINA
Water moderately, allowing the top 2 cm (¾ in) to dry out between waterings.

20 KNOWING WHEN TO WATER

Only water a plant if you are sure that it needs it – and never as a matter of routine. If you cannot tell when a plant needs watering just by looking at it or by feeling the potting mixture, buy a moisture gauge that indicates clearly how moist the potting mixture is. Cheaper, but equally effective, are indicator sticks that change colour according to the moisture content of the potting mixture. If in doubt, wait for a few days before watering.

△ MOISTURE GAUGE
The dial records moisture content on a scale of 1–4.

△ LIGHT/MOISTURE METER
This digital meter gives a more detailed range of light/moisture levels.

△ INDICATOR STICKS
A change in colour shows that watering is required.

21 CHECKING WATER TEMPERATURE

It is best to use tepid water, or at least water at room temperature for watering house plants. Stand a can of water indoors overnight before watering your house plants, to avoid the shock of receiving cold water.

WATERING CAN

22 WHICH IS THE BEST WATER?

Tap water is safe for most plants, but if it has a high lime content boil it first then cool it, particularly before using on lime-hating plants such as azaleas. (Distilled water is lime-free but expensive.) Rain water is excellent if you live in the country, but in towns it is likely to be polluted. Do not use water that has been filtered through a water softener, as the chemicals in the filter can cause serious damage.

23 TOPWATERING

Pour the water directly onto the potting mixture with a narrow-spouted watering can, being careful not to pour water on the leaves and throwing away any excess water that drains through into the drip saucer. Topwatering offers control over the amount of water you give your plant, and allows excess mineral salts that have accumulated in the potting mixture to be flushed out.

TOPWATERING A DRAGON TREE

Avoid wetting leaves

WATERING AN AFRICAN VIOLET

24 WATERING PLANTS FROM BELOW

Some plants, such as cyclamens and African violets, are liable to rot if they get water on their leaves and crowns. Water these from below by filling the drip saucer with water. Leave the plant to soak up what it needs; once the surface is moist, discard any water left in the saucer.

25 HOW TO WATER A BROMELIAD

Most bromeliads have a central cup-like rosette; keep this filled with fresh water, except when the flower bud first appears, and change the water once a month. Water the potting mixture when it dries out, but never overwater, and ensure that there is good drainage.

With non-cup bromeliads, keep the compost moist but never wet.

FILL BROMELIAD CUP WITH WATER

MIND-YOUR-OWN-BUSINESS

26 SYMPTOMS OF UNDERWATERING

Primulas, selaginellas, and plants with succulent stems, such as painted nettles and busy Lizzies, are intolerant of dry conditions and collapse very rapidly. The signs of underwatering are easy to recognize, however:

- The potting mixture shrinks away from the sides of the pot, so that water runs through quickly.
- Leaves become limp and wilt.
- Lower leaves curl, turn yellow, and may drop prematurely.
- Leaves become brown and dried-out looking at the edges.
- Flowers fade and fall quickly.

27 SIGNS OF OVER-WATERING

The worst effects of overwatering take some time to appear, but early signs include yellowing leaves, leaf drop, and poor growth. Later on, soft, rotten patches may begin to develop on leaves, flowers become mouldy, and the roots rot away. A growth of green moss on top of the potting mixture is a sure sign, as moss will grow only in a constantly wet medium.

- To rescue an overwatered, water-logged plant, remove it from its pot and repot in fresh potting mixture; the mixture should contain at least 25 per cent sand to assist drainage.

Green moss on surface

Plant left sitting in water

Stem has collapsed

28 HOW TO REVIVE A PARCHED PLANT

Drooping leaf and flower stalks due to parching

When a plant is very dried out, the potting mixture often becomes quite compacted and difficult for water to penetrate; it also tends to shrink away from the sides of the pot.

If you find a house plant in such a condition, try to revive it with this emergency treatment. If your efforts fail, however, don't discard the plant: just cut back the top growth and wait till it grows again the following year.

CYCLAMEN PERSICUM HYBRID

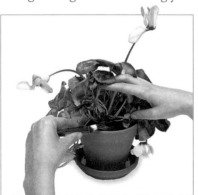

1 Break up dried-out potting mixture with small fork to enable water to penetrate. Be careful not to injure roots.

2 Immerse pot in bowl of water till air bubbles cease rising. Spray leaves. Drain and leave in cool place to revive.

29 WATERING HOUSE PLANTS IN WINTER

Most house plants need a period of rest during the year when watering must be reduced or even stopped altogether. The rest period is brought on by the reduction in available light at certain periods of the year. Giving too much water at this time encourages plant growth that is not, however, supported by adequate light, resulting in poor and mouldy growth, browning of the leaves, and early leaf fall.

30 USING CAPILLARY MATTING

Capillary mats, made of thick felt, can provide your house plants with water when you go away. Place the plants (ideally in plastic pots with several drainage holes) on one end of the moist matting. Leave the other end in a tray or sink full of water. The plants will take up the water they need by capillary action.

Matting trails in water tray

WATERING BY CAPILLARY ACTION

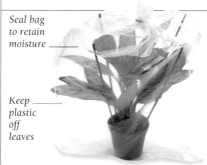

Seal bag to retain moisture

Keep plastic off leaves

SHORT-TERM MOISTURE RETENTION

31 COVERING WITH PLASTIC BAGS

To minimize water loss during a short absence, water your plant thoroughly, leave it to drain, then place in a large, sealed plastic bag, using canes to prevent the leaves touching the sides of the bag. Do not use this method for a long period as the plant may start to rot.

32 MAKING A SELF-WATERING WICK

For a temporary self-watering device, place one end of a length of narrow absorbent material, such as a cotton shoe-lace or an oil-lamp wick, into a water reservoir next to the plant. Push the other end of the wick into the potting mixture and the plant will take up the water it needs.

TEMPORARY PLANT WATERING
The water reservoir will provide water for several plants during a short absence.

Leaves show no signs of wilting

Shoe-lace wick

FEEDING YOUR PLANTS

33 WHY HOUSE PLANTS NEED FEEDING

The potting mixture in which house plants grow has a limited supply of minerals, and once these are used up they must be replaced by feeding. With peat-based mixtures this will be about 6–8 weeks after purchase or repotting; richer loam mixtures last longer before extra feeding is required.

ELEMENTS OF PLANT FEEDING
Given an adequate supply of light, water, and minerals, plants manufacture their own food.

HEALTHY PLANTS

34 RECOGNIZING A HUNGRY PLANT

Plants require three essential minerals: nitrogen for healthy leaf and stem growth, particularly at the start of the growing season; phosphorus for the production of healthy roots and flower buds; and potassium for sturdiness and the development of flowers, fruit, and bulbs. A mineral deficiency can be detected by the following signs:

- Unhealthy "washed-out" look.
- Very slow – or lack of – growth.
- Lowered resistance to diseases and pest infestations.
- Small, pale leaves, occasionally showing yellow spotting.
- Small, poorly coloured flowers, or absence of flowers.
- Weak, spindly stems.
- Dropping of lower leaves.

35 SIGNS OF OVER-FEEDING

Giving a plant too much fertilizer, or applying it at the wrong time, is just as damaging as giving too little. Feed only during a plant's active growing period, using the strength suggested on the label. As a general rule, three feeds of any standard fertilizer applied over the active growing period is quite adequate to keep most house plants healthy.

Scorched edges on leaves

White deposit over surface of potting mixture

White deposit on clay pot

Unhealthy dark patch

OVER-FEEDING DAMAGE
This plant (Philodendron scandens) shows typical signs of overfeeding on the leaves and the surface of the potting mixture.

36 CHOOSING THE RIGHT FERTILIZER

Fertilizers are available in many forms: powders and granules are dissolved in water and applied in the course of normal watering. Similarly, concentrated liquid feeds are diluted in water and watered in. Spikes, pins, and fertilizer pills are placed in the potting mixture and left to release their nutrients slowly when the plant is watered. These, however, can create "hot spots" of concentrated fertilizer, which can burn nearby roots.

SPIKES

SOLUBLE POWDER

LIQUID

PILLS

37 APPLYING LIQUID FERTILIZER

Apply liquid fertilizer (and soluble powders or granules) when you give a plant its usual watering, adding the fertilizer to the water in the recommended strength; for a foliar feed, apply with a sprayer.

WATERING IN LIQUID FERTILIZER
Make sure potting mixture is moist before feeding, to minimize risk of root damage.

APPLYING FOLIAR FEED
For rapid improvement of unhealthy foliage, mist-spray with liquid fertilizer.

38 SLOW-RELEASE FERTILIZERS

Once inserted in the potting mixture, pills and spikes gradually release their food when the plant is watered. The advantage of spikes is that they are easily removed if you think the plant is being overfed.

SLOW-RELEASE FERTILIZER SPIKES
Push the spike in at the edge of the pot and water well to help dissolve the food.

INSERTING FERTILIZER PILL
Push the pill deep into the potting mixture, taking care to avoid damaging the roots.

POTS, POTTING, & POTTING ON

39 POTS & SAUCERS

The main difference between clay and plastic pots – apart from cost and aesthetics – is their porosity: plants grown in clay pots dry out more quickly than those in plastic pots. If you wish to use a container without a drainage hole, put a layer of drainage material in the base.

△ PLASTIC POT & SAUCER
Plants in plastic pots need less frequent watering.

△ LONG TOM

△ GLAZED POT

△ 16 CM (6 IN) POT

△ 12 CM (5 IN) POT

△ SMALL TERRACOTTA TROUGH

△ DECORATIVE TERRACOTTA CONTAINERS
Unglazed pots are not waterproof, so do not put them directly on wooden surfaces.

△ 10 CM (4 IN) POT

△ CLAY HALF-POT

△ TRADITIONAL CLAY POTS
Clay pots and matching saucers (glazed or unglazed) are sold in a range of sizes.

29

40 PREPARING CONTAINERS FOR USE

Before re-using a container, whether it is made of terracotta, plastic, ceramic, or metal, remove the old potting mixture, scrub the pot thoroughly with a solution of disinfectant, then rinse with clean water. This should eliminate any traces of pests or disease that may be present. Clay pots are extremely porous, so before using a new one give it a good soaking in a bucket of cold water, leaving it there until air bubbles stop rising. Saturating the pot helps to prevent moisture being absorbed immediately from the potting mixture and the plant.

SHARDS ▷
Place shards, concave-side down, in the base of the pot to help water drain through.

◁ GRAVEL
Rinse gravel to make sure it is clean before using as drainage material.

41 PROVIDE PROPER DRAINAGE

Improve drainage in plant pots by putting a layer of gravel, pebbles, aggregate, or shards in the bottom before adding the potting mixture. It is especially important to provide drainage in containers that do not have drainage holes in the bottom. When using a clay pot with just one hole in the base, place a single shard across the hole; this will stop the potting mixture being washed out, without hindering drainage.

42 FORK & TROWEL

Keep a set of tools specifically for working on your house plants, as tools that have been used in the garden might introduce damaging diseases or pests to your house-plant collection.

Always choose good quality tools and keep them scrupulously clean. As well as a full-sized trowel, a miniature fork and trowel are handy for working in the limited space around a house plant.

Miniature fork for indoor gardening

Small-scale stainless-steel trowel

43 POTTING MIXTURES

Grow house plants in a ready-prepared potting mixture that has been specifically designed for the purpose, and sterilized to eliminate pests and disease. Two types are available – soil-based and peat-based. The former contains a large proportion of loam, which will supply nutrients for a long period. (Loam is heavy and suitable for larger plants.) Peat-based mixtures are lighter and cleaner to handle, but contain only a limited supply of nutrients, so regular feeding must start after a few weeks to provide the plant with nutrients.

△ SPHAGNUM MOSS
Line a hanging basket with moss as it has excellent water-retentive properties.

△ PERLITE
Perlite granules will improve the drainage and texture of potting mixture.

△ AGGREGATE
Use expanded clay pebbles for drainage or in a pebble tray to improve humidity.

△ WOOD CHARCOAL
A little charcoal prevents acidity, helping to keep the potting mixture sweet.

△ CACTUS COMPOST
Specially formulated from natural ingredients for the slow release of nutrients.

△ HOUSE PLANT COMPOST
A lightweight, peat-based potting mixture containing lime and a wetting agent.

△ COIR BULB FIBRE
A peat-free mixture, made completely from coir fibre to provide good drainage.

44 TAKING OUT A SMALL PLANT

Young, healthy plants soon fill their pots with roots; these then start to grow through the holes in the bottom of the pot, indicating that it is time to pot the plant on.

To make it easier to remove a delicate plant from its pot without causing any root damage, water it an hour beforehand. Take care not to crush fragile leaves and stems.

1 Check plant (here *Chlorophytum comosum* "Vittatum") for signs of roots appearing through drainage hole.

2 Water plant one hour beforehand. Place hand over surface of potting mixture, with stem between fingers.

3 Turn plant upside down, keeping palm of hand over potting mixture. Tap pot gently to loosen root ball.

4 Carefully slide plant and root ball out of pot into your hand, trying not to damage roots growing through holes.

45 TAKING OUT A LARGE PLANT

Enlist help when you have to remove a large plant from its pot: the task will be easier, and the risk of damage to the plant minimized.

- Water plant one hour beforehand.
- Cover floor with old newspapers.
- Run long knife round inner edge of pot to loosen potting mixture.

YUCCA ELEPHANTIPES

1 Supporting plant with one hand, lay pot on its side. Rotate pot slowly, tapping all round with block of wood.

2 When plant is loose, remove from pot: hold steady with both hands while assistant pulls pot away.

USE PAPER BAND TO AVOID PRICKLES

46 HOW TO HANDLE PRICKLY PLANTS

Avoid handling cacti directly as the spines are sharp and many varieties exude an irritating substance.

To remove a cactus from its pot, fold a length of brown paper into a band 4.5 cm (1¾ in) wide. Wrap the band around the cactus and hold the ends in one hand. Pull the pot away with the other hand.

47 POTTING ON

Potting on means moving a plant to a larger pot, and is done at the beginning of a plant's growing season: if you pot on while a plant is resting, no new roots will grow and the extra potting mixture will become waterlogged. Do not feed plants for four to six weeks after potting on, to encourage them to send out new roots to find food.

1 Although *Nolinia recurvata* thrives in a small pot, the protruding roots here indicate that it is time to pot on.

2 Remove plant from pot, supporting stem and root ball. Gently scrape off top surface of old potting mixture.

3 Line base of new pot with crocks or other drainage material, then cover with layer of moist potting mixture.

4 Place plant in new pot and fill in gaps around sides of root ball with potting compost, firming in gently.

48 REPOTTING

Potting on each spring is not necessary for all house plants; some actually thrive in a slightly small pot. If you have checked the roots and the plant shows no sign of being pot-bound, replace it in the same container, but add some fresh potting mixture.

Repotting is also appropriate if you want to curtail the growth of a plant. In this case, remove the plant from its pot and gently crumble away some of the old potting mixture from the root ball. Put the plant in a clean container of the same size and fill around the edges with fresh potting mixture, packing it in firmly.

1 As this *Dracaena congesta* is not pot-bound, it just needs to be repotted with fresh potting mixture. Water well one hour beforehand to ease removal.

2 Remove plant from pot. With fork or fingers, gently scrape away old potting mixture around sides of root ball, taking care not to damage roots.

3 Scrub pot thoroughly and place layer of drainage material in bottom. Insert plant and fill around edges with fresh potting mixture, firming in gently.

49 WHEN TO TOPDRESS

If a plant is too large to be potted on easily, or if it does not like having its roots disturbed, provide a fresh supply of nutrients by topdressing.

GRAPE IVY ▷
Topdress large specimens.

◁ SCREW PINE
Top-dress older plants if required.

△ **KENTIA PALM**
Once a plant is in a 30 cm (12 in) pot, topdress.

1 Gently scrape away the top few centimetres of the potting mixture with a small fork, being careful not to damage the roots or stem of the plant.

2 Refill the pot to its original level with fresh potting mixture. Firm down so that the plant (here *Dracaena marginata*) is securely anchored.

PRUNING & TRAINING

50 USEFUL TOOLS & EQUIPMENT

You need very few special tools for pruning and training house plants. A pair of scissors is fine for pruning soft stems, but you will need a pair of sharp secateurs for thicker, woody stems. Supports and ties are required for climbing plants.

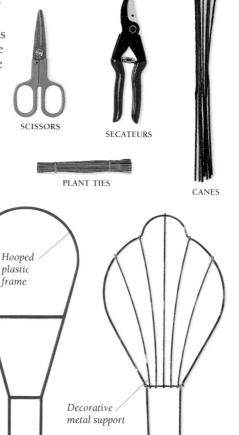

SCISSORS

SECATEURS

PLANT TIES

CANES

Hooped plastic frame

Decorative metal support

TRAINING SUPPORTS △ ▷
As well as simple bamboo canes, you can obtain plastic and metal shapes to train plants around.

51 WHEN TO PRUNE

The best time to prune is spring when active new growth begins, but overlong stems can be trimmed back in the autumn if necessary. Prune to thin out tangled growth, to improve a plant's overall shape, and to limit the size of a plant that has become too big.

HOW TO CUT ▷
Cut, sloping down, from just above a bud, along the line indicated.

Cut above outward-facing bud

PRUNING INTO SHAPE △
This weeping fig (Ficus benjamina) *is being pruned to improve its shape.*

52 DEADHEADING FLOWERING PLANTS

Deadheading (cutting away dead or faded flowers on a plant) encourages the plant to continue producing more flowers instead of putting its energy into generating seeds, as it would naturally do.

REMOVING FLOWERS ON LONG STALKS
With plants like Tom thumb (Kalanchoe blossfeldiana), *cut out the whole stalk from the base, not just the flower head.*

DEADHEADING FLOWERS ON SHORT STALKS
Pinch out flowers on short stalks, such as this jasmine (Jasminum polyanthum), *between your thumb and index finger.*

53 CUTTING BACK STRAGGLY GROWTH

Fast-growing climbers, such as jasmine (*Jasminum polyanthum*) or grape ivy (*Cissus rhombifolia*), which are often trained around hoops and canes, need to be pruned back if their growth becomes straggly, in order to encourage a better shape and bushier growth. In early spring, cut out all but the newest growth; in a very short time the plant will be covered with new shoots.

Stem needs cutting back

JASMINUM POLYANTHUM ▷
Although they look delicate, jasmines need drastic pruning of their vigorous growth.

1 When growth becomes straggly and unattractive, unwind stems from support. Cut out all old stems from base of plant and prune straggly new shoots.

2 Wind remaining stems round wire support and secure with wire ties. Though pruning appears drastic, strong new shoots will develop rapidly.

54 PINCHING TIPS FOR BUSHY GROWTH

Pinch out the tips on plants with long unbranched stems, such as Swedish ivy (*Plectranthus australis*) to encourage the production of side shoots and to give the plant a bushier appearance. Pinching out also prevents climbers and trailers from becoming too straggly, and helps to increase the number of flower buds on flowering plants.

Nip out tips of young plants

PINCH OUT GROWING TIPS

55 GROWING A STANDARD

Although fairly unusual, it is easy to train a house plant as a standard – an elegantly formal tall plant with a bare stem. As well as the Chinese hibiscus (*Hibiscus rosa-sinensis*) shown here, you could also train a geranium or fuchsia.

1 Select vigorous young plant; if there is more than one stem, retain strongest-looking one.

2 Remove side shoots, leaving foliage. When plant is of desired height, pinch out growing tips.

STANDARD HIBISCUS

56 SUPPORTS FOR CLIMBING PLANTS

Always use the appropriate support for your climbing plants. Those with aerial roots, such as a Swiss cheese plant (*Monstera deliciosa*), benefit from a moss pole to provide extra moisture. Wire hoops are ideal for climbers with several stems; formed into a balloon shape, they allow good circulation of air. Twining plants and those with tendrils grow easily up a bamboo tripod, though they may need to be tied in initially. A single-stemmed plant needs only a central bamboo cane for support.

NATURAL SUPPORT
Cape leadwort (Plumbago auriculata) scrambles over the basket's handle.

SIMPLE WIRE HOOPS
Jasminum officinale *here grows over two hoops. Add more hoops if necessary.*

SINGLE CANE STAKE
Insert cane before planting (here Ficus benjamina) to avoid damaging roots.

BAMBOO TRIPOD
Twine Trachelospermum jasminoides *around cane tripod, tying in stems.*

57 MAKING A FRESH MOSS POLE

A moss pole provides perfect support for a climbing plant as well as a constantly moist medium for aerial roots to cling to. You can buy moss poles, but homemade poles are better as they hold more moist moss. To make a pole, you need a 50 x 18 cm (20 x 7 in) rectangle of chicken wire, two bamboo sticks, some sphagnum moss, and wire.

1 Roll chicken wire into tube shape. Join long edges by twisting loose ends securely together.

2 Form cross support with two bamboo canes. Lash together; fix to tube; wedge into pot.

3 Two-thirds fill pot with potting mixture. Fill wire tube with moss, packing down with stick.

4 Pot up plants around base of tube; attach stems to pole; water moss and potting mixture well.

KEEP IT MOIST
Put pot in warm shady position. Keep potting compost and moss pole constantly moist (here Philodendron scandens*).*

PROPAGATING HOUSE PLANTS

58 USEFUL EQUIPMENT

Whether you choose the vegetative method of propagating house plants (taking cuttings) or intend to grow from seed, you do not need much special equipment. However, a propagation tray or, more simply, a clear plastic bag secured around a pot, is useful as either will provide the humid atmosphere that encourages the rapid germination of seeds and helps cuttings to root more quickly.

△ PROPAGATION TRAY

△ PLASTIC POT

△ PEAT POT

△ KNIFE

△ SCISSORS

PLANT △ TIES

RUBBER △ BANDS

△ PENCIL & LABELS   △ DIBBER   △ CLEAR PLASTIC BAGS

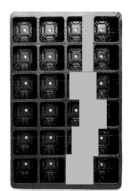

△ PLASTIC TRAY

△ PEAT TRAY

59 WHY USE ROOTING HORMONES?

Taking stem cuttings is one of the most common methods of house plant propagation, and getting the cuttings to root quickly is vital, as the longer it takes, the greater the chance of the stem rotting. Rooting hormones help the rooting process by supplementing the supply of natural hormones (auxins) that accumulate in the base of a cutting.

Liquid rooting solution

Hormone rooting powder

SYNTHETIC ROOTING HORMONES

60 ROOTING CUTTINGS IN WATER

This is the simplest method of rooting softwood cuttings. Take the cuttings in early spring from a healthy, vigorous plant, choosing new, short-noded side shoots, and remove each cutting just above a node. When preparing cuttings, always use a sharp knife and make clean, precise cuts so that no snags are left on the parent plant. Keep the cuttings in a light, warm place until the new roots appear.

1 With sharp knife trim cutting (here *Coleus blumei*) below node; remove all lower leaves.

2 Insert stems through wire net over jar of water, ensuring stems are in water. Keep topped up.

3 When cuttings are well rooted, plant in 6 cm (2½ in) pots of sandy potting compost.

61 ROOTING IN COMPOST

Root softwood cuttings in cutting compost, a free-draining mixture, often based on bark or perlite, with a high percentage of coarse sand. Dip the ends of the cuttings in hormone rooting powder to speed up the root development and plant around the edge of the pot. Cutting compost is low in nutrients so feed the cuttings once they are rooted.

1 Fill clean 12 cm (5 in) plastic pot with moist cutting compost. Pack down compost until it is firm and level.

2 With secateurs or sharp knife, cut off some new, short-noded shoots above node (here *Gynura aurantiaca*).

3 With sharp knife, trim each cutting below node. Remove lower leaves from stem; take care to leave no snags.

4 Dip ends of cuttings into hormone rooting powder; using dibber, insert in pot with leaves just above compost.

5 Place in propagator in warm, light place. Maintain soil temperature of 18–21° C (64–70° F) until cuttings root.

62 PROPAGATING FROM CUT LEAVES

House plants can be easily produced from leaf cuttings. Plants with prominent veins on the leaves, such as *Begonia rex-cultorum* (seen here) or *Streptocarpus*, will produce small plantlets if the leaves are cut up or scored and the cut veins kept in contact with the moist compost. With a sharp knife, divide each leaf in half or into smaller sections, or leave whole and score through the veins on the underside of the leaf.

1 Select and remove healthy young leaf from parent plant. Make 1 cm (½ in) long incision straight across strongest veins on underside of leaf.

2 Place prepared leaf, cut-side down, on tray of moist cutting compost. Pin veins to compost. (If using small sections, each must include vein.)

3 Place tray in propagator or in sealed clear plastic bag. Leave tray in warm place, out of direct sunlight. Maintain temperature of 18–24° C (64–75° F).

4 When plantlets have developed from cut veins, carefully lift and separate from leaf. Pot up singly in 6 cm (2½ in) pots filled with potting compost.

63 ROOTING A LEAF WITH STALK

Some plants, especially those with fleshy leaves growing in a rosette shape, such as the African violet (*Saintpaulia*), can be propagated from a complete leaf plus its stalk.

▪ Select a healthy, undamaged leaf, preferably one that is neither too young nor too old.

▪ Cut off the leaf close to the base of the leaf stalk, and trim the stalk with a straight cut approximately 3 cm (1¼ in) below the leaf blade.

▪ Provide a humid atmosphere for the cutting by enclosing in a plastic bag or an improvised cloche.

▪ Remove plastic bag or other cover once the plantlets have developed.

1 Cut healthy leaf from parent plant (here *Saintpaulia* hybrid). Trim stem to 3 cm (1¼ in). Insert in pot of cutting compost, with leaf touching compost.

2 Water pots, label, and cover with clear plastic bags or cloches made from plastic bottle bases. Leave in warm, light place till plantlets develop.

▽ DEVELOPED PLANTLETS
Remove covering and leave in pot until big enough to pot up.

Each leaf produces several plantlets

64 PROPAGATING FROM RUNNERS

Some plants produce plantlets on runners. Root these individually in pots of cutting compost; sever from the parent plant after a few weeks. Shown here *Saxifraga stolonifera*.

PROPAGATE BY ROOTING RUNNERS
Peg down runner in moist compost. Once rooted, sever runner close to young plant.

65 HOW TO LAYER HOUSE PLANTS

Layering involves rooting the stem of a plant that makes aerial roots at the nodes or leaf joints, such as *Philodendron scandens* (seen here) while the stem is still attached.

LAYERING A PHILODENDRON
Peg down stem with bent wire at node. Sever stem once new plant has developed.

66 DIVISION OF OFFSETS

Offsets are small plants that appear around the base of mature plants, including many bromeliads and cacti. Once the offsets are well established, separate them from the parent plant; grow on separately.

1 When offset is well established, with shape and characteristics of parent plant (here *Aechmea*), sever at base with knife, retaining any existing roots.

2 Fill pot with moist rooting mixture. Insert offset so that base stays on surface. Place pot in plastic bag; leave until growth indicates offset is rooted.

67 ROOTSTOCK DIVISION

Many house plants, such as *Calathea* (shown here), *Saintpaulia* hybrids, ferns, and some cacti, can be propagated by carefully dividing up the rootstock, then potting up each section in its own container.

1 Water plant thoroughly one hour before removing from pot. Gently tease or wash away surplus compost until separate root sections are visible.

2 Using hands or hand fork, prise root ball into equal sections, each with portion of roots. Be careful not to damage stems or roots.

3 Trim back any thick roots with clean, sharp knife, so that divisions fit into new pots. Be particularly careful to leave delicate fibrous roots intact.

POT UP DIVISIONS
Insert sections in moist, loam-based potting compost. Water well and label.

68 Growing house plants from seed

You can grow many popular house plants from seed. It is vital for successful germination that the growing medium is kept constantly moist, but not too wet, and at the correct temperature – at least 15° C (59° F), but much higher for sub-tropical and tropical plants. Check the packet for advice on whether to germinate in the dark or the light.

1 To help sow very fine seeds evenly, mix first in bag with some dry fine sand. (Sow larger seeds individually.)

2 Sow seed mixture thinly from paper scoop onto pot of moist rooting mixture. Label and place in propagator.

3 When seedlings are big enough to handle, prick out with dibber and sow in tray of moist potting compost.

4 Once seedlings have developed at least two true leaves, pot on into individual pots. Avoid handling stems.

TACKLING PESTS & DISEASES

69 ROUTINE MAINTENANCE

As well as caring for your plants' specific requirements in terms of light, water, humidity, and feeding, try to find time, every two weeks or so, to clean and inspect them carefully. This will alert you to problems at an early stage and allow you to take immediate remedial action.

Keep one mist sprayer just for applying pesticides

70 AVOID DISEASE

Regularly remove all damaged and yellowing leaves, cutting them off close to the base; leaving them on the plant tends to encourage disease or pests. For the same reason, remove all faded flowers and, once the individual blooms have finished flowering, remove the entire flower stalk also. Leaving sections of flower stalk can cause rotting in the centre of the plant.

REMOVE DEAD LEAVES
The dead leaves on this Boston fern (Nephrolepis exaltata "Bostoniensis") may be due to a dry atmosphere. Pinch out the affected leaves and stems and increase humidity.

71 KEEPING HOUSE PLANTS CLEAN

House plants inevitably get dusty and you must clean them regularly, not just because dusty leaves are unattractive, but because they also hinder the plant's ability to absorb sunlight, water, and carbon dioxide.

Clean your plants by whichever method is most appropriate, but, if you get the chance, put your house plants outside in a gentle shower of rain when the weather is mild for a refreshing and effective cleansing.

CLEANING A PLANT WITH HAIRY LEAVES
Brush away dust on a hairy-leaved plant with a small, soft, dry paintbrush.

WIPING LARGE-LEAVED PLANTS
Support the leaf with one hand and gently wipe it clean with a damp cloth or sponge.

CLEANING SMALL-LEAVED PLANTS
Put a large plant with small leaves in the bath and gently spray it with tepid water.

72 SYSTEMIC & CONTACT INSECTICIDES

Systemic insecticides contain chemicals that are absorbed by the plant through its leaves or roots; these destroy leaf-eating and sap-sucking pests without harming the plant itself. Contact insecticides are sprayed directly onto the pests, and kill them directly. Insecticides are available as liquids, sprays, dust, granules, or in handy aerosol cans.

73 COMMON DISEASES

Although house plants are not prone to disease, overwatering produces the conditions in which bacteria thrive, as does failure to remove damaged leaves and stems. Pests transmit diseases and weaken plants, making them vulnerable.

Remedial action is essential when a problem does occur: remove all diseased sections immediately and isolate the plant during treatment.

SOOTY MOULD
This looks like a thick layer of sticky soot, and indicates that the plant is infested with sap-sucking pests. Wash off the mould with soapy water, and identify and treat the plant for the pests responsible.

GREY MOULD (BOTRYTIS)
This disease, which results in a fluffy-grey, mouldy appearance, affects plants with soft stems and leaves, and strikes when the temperature is low and the air moist. Treat with a suitable fungicide.

MILDEW (POWDERY MILDEW)
Mildew causes powdery white patches on the leaves, which then become distorted or drop. Soft-leaved and succulent-stemmed plants are susceptible. Pick off affected leaves and spray plant with fungicide.

BLACKLEG
Blackleg, which mainly affects geraniums, occurs when the potting mixture is kept too wet. There is no cure, so prevent the problem by using free-draining potting mixture and avoiding overwatering.

STEM, ROOT, & CROWN ROT
Low temperatures and saturated potting mixture encourage stem, root, or crown rot, the affected areas appearing soft and slimy. Cut out rotting sections and apply fungicide. Root rot is usually fatal.

74 IDENTIFYING HOUSE PLANT PESTS

Although house plants are less likely to be attacked by pests than garden plants, they can suffer serious damage if an attack is not treated. Inspect new plants for signs of pests before bringing them into your home; once there, check them regularly and deal promptly with any infestation. Treat any mild attack by washing the plant with soapy water; if the problem is more serious, identify the pest and treat the plant with a suitable insecticide. Some pests attack only certain plants while others, such as whiteflies and aphids, are less discriminating.

APHIDS

Often known as "greenflies", aphids can also be black, brown, grey, or light yellow. Their moulted white cases are often found on infested plants. Aphids suck sap and exude a sticky substance on which sooty mould can grow. Treat with a contact spray or, if the attack is severe, a systemic insecticide.

PLANTS AT RISK
All plants with soft stems and soft leaves, e.g. busy Lizzies.

FUNGUS GNATS (SCIARID FLIES)

These tiny, sluggish insects exist in all peat and peat-based mixtures. They hover above the surface of the potting mixture, in which they lay their eggs. The larvae feed on dead matter, and may attack the roots of seedlings. Treat by drenching the potting mixture with an insecticide when it is dry.

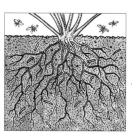

ADULT

LARVA

PLANTS AT RISK
Plants in peat-based compost.

MEALY BUGS & ROOT MEALY BUGS

Oval-shaped and about 0.5 cm (¼ in) long, mealy bugs resemble woodlice, and are covered in a sticky white wax that repels water. They are sap-suckers and exude a sticky honeydew, causing leaf fall. Treat by drenching the potting mixture with systemic insecticide at two-weekly intervals.

PLANTS AT RISK
Cacti, African violets, and geraniums are all vulnerable.

RED SPIDER MITE

Barely visible to the naked eye, these sap-suckers can be detected by the fine, silky webs they spin on the undersides of leaves and around leaf axils. Their presence causes mottling of leaves, stunted growth, and leaf drop. Treat a severe attack by spraying upper and lower leaf surfaces with insecticide.

PLANTS AT RISK
Plants growing under cover in hot, dry air.

SCALE INSECTS

Brown or yellowish in colour, scale insects are usually found on the lower surface of leaves. Adult females remain stationary, enclosed in waxy covers, and appear as circular or oval raised discs. They are sap-suckers and exude a sticky honeydew, causing sooty mould. Treat with a systemic insecticide.

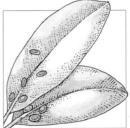

PLANTS AT RISK
Ferns and the citrus family are susceptible to infestation.

WHITEFLIES

These tiny, white, moth-like creatures are usually found in the greenhouse or conservatory, and are brought in with temporary flowering plants, such as geraniums. They suck sap and exude a sticky honeydew, and are found on the undersides of leaves. Treat with both a spray insecticide and a systemic type.

PLANTS AT RISK
Flowering plants brought in from the greenhouse are vulnerable.

VINE WEEVILS

Adult weevils are large and almost black in colour; the grubs are cream-coloured. The adults bite pieces out of leaves, while the grubs eat roots, tubers, and corms, resulting in plant collapse. There is no remedy if the root system has been destroyed, but for less severe attacks, drench the compost with insecticide.

PLANTS AT RISK
Rosette-shaped succulents are the most likely to be affected.

75 IDENTIFYING PROBLEMS

Most house-plant problems are caused by too much or too little water, light, humidity, and heat. However, if correctly identified, the problem can usually be rectified and the plant restored to health.

Pale, spindly growth usually due to lack of light; cut back leggy growth to encourage bushiness, and move to brighter position

Loss of variegated colouring in leaves caused by inadequate light; move plant to more brightly lit position

Brown patch on leaf caused by too much sun; provide some form of shade or move plant away from window

Curling leaf edges often indicate that lighting is too bright; move house plant to shadier position

Rotting leaves and stems due to fungal disease that occurs in poor growing conditions; remove all affected parts and make sure that plant is not overwatered

Dried-up lower leaves and leaf drop due to poor light, too much heat, or lack of water; move house plant to brighter position, away from direct source of heat, and water as required

Leaf drop usually caused by draught, sudden drop in temperature, or dryness of roots; move plant to more sheltered position and water as necessary

Poor light may cause lack of flowers; move plant to brighter position

Flowers often drop rapidly if temperature is too high and atmosphere dry; set plant on moist pebble tray to increase humidity around it

Brown leaf tips and margins usually due to dry air; mist-spray plant regularly and improve humidity by placing on moist pebble tray

Wilting leaves may be due to too much or too little water. If potting mixture is very dry, soak pot in bowl of water for half an hour; if very wet, repot into barely moist potting mixture

Yellowing leaves and leaf drop usually caused by cold draughts; move plant to more sheltered position

FAVOURITE HOUSE PLANTS

76 POINSETTIA

(Euphorbia pulcherrima)
It is not easy to get poinsettias to bloom for a second year, so treat them as temporary plants and discard when they are past their best. Put the plant in a cool room to prolong its decorative period; avoid over-watering, which causes leaf fall.

Vividly coloured bracts

Remove flowerheads as they fade

77 REGAL GERANIUM

(Pelargonium domesticum hybrids)* The regal geranium flowers from spring till midsummer. Remove faded flower heads regularly and feed occasionally with liquid fertilizer. When flowering is over, prune the plant back by at least half. Water the plant sparingly in winter and repot, in spring, in a soil-based potting mixture.

FAVOURITE HOUSE PLANTS

78 SPIDER PLANT

(Chlorophytum comosum
"Vittatum")* Allow a 3 cm (1¼ in)
space at the top of the pot for the
emergence of this plant's thick,
white roots. Feed it fortnightly
and repot in spring, with soil-
based potting mixture, if the
roots have filled the pot.

*Leaves grow to
60 cm (24 in)*

79 RUBBER PLANT

(Ficus elastica) Clean older
leaves regularly with a damp cloth,
but do not touch delicate younger
leaves. Topdress a large old plant
once it becomes impractical to pot
on into a bigger container.

*Clean leaves
allow plant
to function
efficiently*

80 PARLOUR PALM

(Chamaedorea elegans
"Bella")* These dwarf palms, which
reach a height of 90 cm (36 in),
flourish in warm, moist conditions.
Small plants are ideal for planting
in bottle gardens and terraria.

*Repot in
spring, but
only if roots
fill pot*

81 BOSTON FERN

(Nephrolepis exaltata "Bostoniensis") This fern requires high humidity, so stand it on a moist pebble tray and spray-mist regularly. Water plentifully during the active growing period.

Tips die if air is too dry

82 MOTHER-IN-LAW'S TONGUE

(Sansevieria trifasciata "Laurentii") When roots appear on the surface, repot using a mixture of one-third coarse sand and two-thirds of soil-based potting mixture.

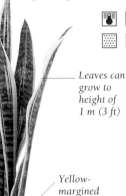

Leaves can grow to height of 1 m (3 ft)

Yellow-margined leaves emerge from below-surface stem

83 SWISS CHEESE PLANT

(Monstera deliciosa) Train this plant around a moss-pole, and tuck the long, thick aerial roots into either the moss or the potting mixture. Never cut off aerial roots as they absorb nutrients for the plant.

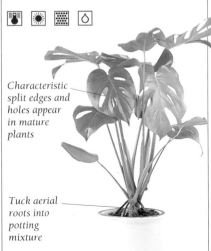

Characteristic split edges and holes appear in mature plants

Tuck aerial roots into potting mixture

84 HYACINTH
(Hyacinthus orientalis)
Plant the bulbs close together in a bowl of bulb fibre or soil-based potting mixture, leaving the tips protruding. Winter "prepared" bulbs for six weeks, ordinary bulbs for ten, in a cool, dark place.

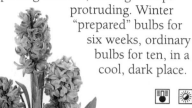

Provide support for tall stems if necessary

85 AFRICAN VIOLET
(Saintpaulia hybrids)
Feed regularly throughout the year with specially prepared African violet liquid fertilizer, used at one-quarter strength. When the roots fill the pot, repot with a mixture of peat moss, perlite, and vermiculite.

Avoid wetting leaves when watering

86 PAINTED-LEAF BEGONIA
(Begonia rex-cultorum) Also known as rex begonias, these plants are grown for the beautiful colour and interesting texture of their leaves.

Plants can grow to 30 cm (12 in) high

87 AZALEA
(Rhododendron simsii) Treat azaleas as annuals and discard after flowering. To prolong flowering period, keep moist and display plant in a cool location.

Mist-spray leaves, avoiding flowers

88 WINTER CHERRY
(Solanum capsicastrum)
To keep these plants for a second fruiting season, cut away half the growth and move them outside in 12 cm (5 in) pots for the summer

Berries are poisonous, so keep away from children

89 FLORIST'S CHRYSANTHEMUM
(Chrysanthemum morifolium hybrids) Cultivated to grow no more than 30 cm (12 in) high, these plants are best treated as annuals. If buying a plant, check that the buds show colour, as tight green buds often fail to open.

Keep compost moist to prolong flowering

90 BUSY LIZZIE
(Impatiens wallerana hybrids) Busy Lizzies are fast-growing and can reach a height of 35 cm (14 in). To encourage bushy growth, pinch out the plant's growing tips. Repot in spring, but only if the roots have completely filled the existing pot.

Mist-spray leaves

91 FLORIST'S CYCLAMEN
(Cyclamen persicum hybrids) Never pour water directly onto the tuber: moisten by immersing the pot in water for 15 minutes.

Remove flowers as they die

92 ENGLISH IVY

(Hedera helix) English ivy hybrids, available in a range of leaf colours and shapes, can grow large and straggly, so pinch out the tips to encourage bushiness. Stand the pots on moist pebble trays to increase humidity.

Variegated leaves need good light

93 TRADESCANTIA

(Tradescantia albiflora "Albovittata") This fast-growing plant is very easy to propagate by taking stem cuttings, so discard a plant after its second repotting and replace with a younger one. Pinch out the tips to aid bushy growth, and display the plant as a trailer or climber.

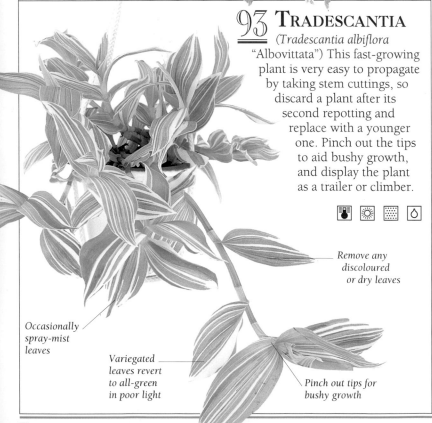

Remove any discoloured or dry leaves

Occasionally spray-mist leaves

Variegated leaves revert to all-green in poor light

Pinch out tips for bushy growth

Aerial root
seeks out
moisture

Leaves
darken
with age

94 HEARTLEAF PHILODENDRON

(Philodendron scandens) This is a fast-growing plant, ideal for training up a moss pole – the aerial roots will grow into the moss, which must be kept constantly moist. Set pot on a moist pebble tray to increase humidity.

95 KANGAROO VINE

(Cissus antarctica)
The kangaroo vine
will tolerate dry air,
but if it is in a warm,
stuffy room, increase the
humidity by standing the
pot on a moist pebble tray. If
the plant is growing in a hanging
basket, mist-spray it frequently.

Tendril provides
support when
climbing

Glossy green
leaves with
marked veining
and scalloped edge

CLINGING VINES
*This Australian climbing
plant is a true vine with
the characteristic forked
tendrils that allow it to
cling to supports.*

DISPLAY & ARRANGEMENT

96 THE KEY TO A GOOD ARRANGEMENT

A good plant arrangement is one that balances visually, and this depends on factors such as the relative sizes of plants in the group, and the presence of any eye-catching features. Add an element of contrast to spice up the arrangement.

SHAPE ▷
The spiky queen agave provides a link between the tip yucca and the cacti.

TEXTURE △
The differing textures of the peperomia and the fern balance the difference in size.

COLOUR ▷
The grouping of three pink begonias is balanced by offsetting the single white specimen.

97 THE RIGHT CONTAINER

The ideal container is one that balances the size and shape of a plant. Small plants look best in small pots, but with larger plants you must pay attention to both the overall shape and height of the plant and the container.

Whatever type of container you use, drainage is vital: if a pot does not have a drainage hole, put some crocks in the bottom before adding compost.

This plant likes to be potbound, so the small dish is ideal

SIMPLE TERRACOTTA △
A small plain dish is the perfect foil for the bizarre shape of the weeping ponytail plant.

CONICAL EMPHASIS ▽
The strong outline of these bromeliads continues the crisp lines of the conical glass bowl.

Fronds can grow up to 90 cm (36 in) in length

CLASSICAL FORM △
A lead urn provides a formal setting for the exuberant fronds of a Boston fern.

98 GROUPING PLANTS IN A CONTAINER

Create a spectacular display by grouping together, temporarily, several plants in full flower or with foliage at its best. Select plants that require similar growing conditions, but leave each plant in its own pot.

To recreate this display you need:
- Primulas (*Primula obconica*).
- English ivy (*Hedera helix* hybrids).
- Rush basket, plastic lining, clay pellets, coir.

1 Line basket with plastic. Cut to shape, leaving a small overhang. Cover bottom of basket with layer of clay pellets about 3 cm (1¼ in) deep.

2 Fill basket with 6 cm (2½ in) coir. Place taller primulas at back, ivy trailing over side, and smaller primulas at front. Pack coir firmly around pots.

CARE FOR YOUR DISPLAY
To keep the display looking fresh, position it in cool, filtered sunlight. Remove fading flowers and yellowing leaves, and keep the primulas well watered.

99 GROUPING CONTAINERS

To hold a group of plants and pots together visually, choose pots of similar shape, style, or colour, but of different sizes; or link a group of contrasting pots by having the same type of plant in each one. Enhance a group of colourful foliage plants by displaying them in containers that echo their colouring. Bear in mind the plants' requirements when positioning the display.

Grey ceramic pot

Pothos vine

White pot picks up leaf variegation

Croton

Painted-leaf begonia

Red plastic pot

Mind-your-own-business

Large clay pot

CONTRASTING SIZES △
Using the same plant in both of two contrasting containers helps to hold the group together.

COUNTERPOINT △
The black and red of the containers echoes the leaf colouring of both the begonia and the croton.

LITTLE ECHOES ▷
Unity is achieved in this group by the repetition of container shape and texture.

100 PLANTING A TERRARIUM

The humid atmosphere of terraria suits plants that need plentiful watering and a high level of humidity. Use light, free-draining, moisture-retentive potting mixture over a layer of drainage material. Plant taller plants at the back or centre of the terrarium, then fill out the remaining spaces with smaller, creeping plants.

1 Cover bottom layer of pebbles and charcoal with moistened compost.

2 Remove plants from pots; shake off loose compost; tease out roots.

3 Carefully place plants in chosen positions, leaving space for growth.

4 Fill in around plants with more compost, firming down gently.

5 Cover any bare areas with moss to prevent compost drying out.

6 Lightly spray plants and moss with fine mist of water; replace lid.

101 HANGING BASKET DISPLAY

To recreate the hanging basket shown here you need a wire basket, plastic lining, peat-based potting mixture, sphagnum moss, and some white and blue Italian bellflowers (*Campanula isophylla*), which flower continuously from late summer through autumn.

1 Line basket with 5 cm (2 in) layer of damp moss, overlapped with plastic. Make small holes around base of plastic.

2 Water plants, remove from pots, and divide into smaller sections to push through moss and holes in plastic.

3 Complete planting around base; cover with layer of potting mixture, then plant up sides and top of basket.

4 When basket is full, tuck in excess plastic. Water basket well; secure chains, and hang in sunny place.

INDEX

Acknowledgments

Dorling Kindersley would like to thank
Hilary Bird for compiling the index, Isobel Holland for proof-
reading, and Nick Parritt for invaluable horticultural advice.

Photography
KEY: t *top*; b *bottom*; c *centre*; l *left*; r *right*
All photographs by Matthew Ward, except for: Peter Anderson
18br, 5tr, 41, 44b, 45, 46, 47, 48tl, 48b, 49, 50, 51b, 68; Tom
Dobbie 2, 8, 15, 16, 17, 19, 36tr, 36tl, 36tc, 57, 8; 59, 60
(except tl), 61, 62, 63, 64c, 72; Dave King 12b, 41t, 42,
60tl, 64t, 64b, 65, 66, 67, 69.

Illustrations
David Ashby 53, 54, 55, 56.